Gluten-Free Baking Classics
FOR THE Bread Machine

ANNALISE G. ROBERTS

Gluten-Free
Baking Classics
FOR THE Bread Machine

ANNALISE G. ROBERTS

SURREY BOOKS

AGATE

CHICAGO

All photography © 2008 by Joel Basta

Printed in the United States.

Library of Congress Cataloging-in-Publication Data

Roberts, Annalise G.
  Gluten-free baking classics for the bread machine / Annalise G. Roberts.
      p. cm.
  Includes index.
  Summary: "Recipes and detailed instructions for making gluten-free breads in the bread machine. Includes recipes for gluten-free flour mixes"--Provided by publisher.
  ISBN-13: 978-1-57284-104-8 (pbk.)
  ISBN-10: 1-57284-104-4 (pbk.)
  1. Gluten-free diet--Recipes. 2. Baking. 3. Automatic bread machines. I. Title.
  RM237.86.R583 2009
  641.8'15--dc22
                          2008055258

10 9 8 7 6 5 4 3 2

Surrey Books is an imprint of Agate Publishing. Agate books are available in bulk at discount prices. Single copies are available prepaid direct from the publisher. For more information visit agatepublishing.com.

TABLE OF CONTENTS

Dedication

To Conrad, Alexander, and Bradford

*Who good-naturedly ate huge quantities of grilled cheese, panini,
stuffing, bread pudding, cheese toast, French toast, and cutlets
coated with bread crumbs while I tested recipes for this book.*

Acknowledgments

Thanks to Douglas Seibold, president and publisher of Agate Publishing, for giving me the opportunity to write this cookbook and for all his encouragement and kind prodding to do it sooner, rather than later.

Thanks to Eileen Johnson, executive vice president, global sales, of Agate Publishing, for spearheading the project and for her behind-the-scenes work with Zojirushi.

Thanks to Perrin Davis, senior vice president, editorial services, of Agate Publishing, for helping me craft such a lovely book and for orchestrating the photography sessions.

Thanks to my many willing tasters, especially Alex and Bradford, Herb and Ev, Tim, Monica and Cory, Donald and Pamela, Joan and Nino Carnevale, and last but not least, Carla Krueger.

And it is with much gratitude and appreciation that I thank my field testers for doing such an incredible job in such a relatively small amount of time. They offered up their time, kitchens, and bread machines to test recipes for this book, and I couldn't have done it without them. A huge thank you to Amy Luczak, Jeff Robins, Jen Cross, Jeanne Cobetto, Alison Beck, Claudia Pillow, Perrin Davis, Eileen Johnson, Doris Schapira, Ellen Turcio, Linda Merrill, Jason Dietel, Sue Lampropoulos, Rita Yohalem, and Alexandra Jones.

The Bread Machine Saga

In the past, baking bread was something I did whenever I had extra time, the weather was cool and dry, I had a yearning to work with dough, and I felt hungry for a very specific bread. The memory of its scent and taste would keep running through my mind until I just had to make it stop. Finally, I would give in and plan an entire meal around that one bread, as if that would justify the luxury of making it—because for me, baking bread was a luxury.

But after I was diagnosed with a gluten intolerance, baking bread became a necessity. Unwilling to sacrifice taste, texture, and freshness, I began to develop recipes for the breads I missed. Fortunately, I never ate a lot of bread to begin with, so it wasn't something I felt compelled to turn out assembly line–style in my kitchen. I was more than happy to bake loaves using my mixer and oven. But time and again, readers of my books and students in my classes asked if my recipes could be used with a bread machine. They sought a combination of convenience and delicious gluten-free bread, two things that had previously been mutually exclusive. In truth, I didn't know the answer, because I'd never tried. Finally, the lingering question of whether it could be done *well* prodded me to try.

I must admit that I perched my new bread machine, still in its unopened box, on my fireplace hearth for more than a week; I glared at it daily. Never an early adapter of any technology (after all, hasn't it been 20 years now since bread machines burst onto the scene?), I eventually forced myself to take it out of the box and place it on the kitchen counter.

Like a scientist searching to understand, I played with the controls, filled the pan with a gloppy liquid I made up for the occasion, pressed **Start/Restart**, and watched how the paddles worked (the little window is a big help!). I monitored the temperature of the liquid at the beginning and end of each cycle in order to better understand how the machine functioned. I read the manufacturer's directions about how to put in the ingredients—and then decided to ignore them, because they didn't make any sense to me based on what I knew about how the machine worked and how good gluten-free bread is made. Eventually, I designed a set of commands for the bread machine's **HOME MADE** cycle based on what I thought could work.

I couldn't put it off any longer—it was time to try to bake my first loaf. I started with my very dependable Basic Sandwich Bread recipe, which in its original form makes a 1-pound loaf in an 8½ × 4½-inch pan. Using my mixer and oven, I successfully figured out how to scale the recipe up to bake a 2-pound loaf size that was more suitable for the machine.

Once I had the ingredients right, I programmed the settings and pressed **Start/Restart** on the bread machine. The bread rose beautifully, baked to a golden brown ... and then developed a crater-like center when I took it out. Clearly, I had more to learn—and I did. This book is the result: a well-tested collection of delicious bread recipes you can make in a bread machine. I'm sure you'll find something you like—something you can look forward to making again and again. Perhaps you'll even find a recipe you can plan your own special meal around.

Getting
Started

Baking is part art and part science. It combines careful measurement with creative flavorings and flourishes. My thoughts about gluten-free baking are in harmony with my basic philosophy about all cooking: It should be simple and not all-consuming. This chapter provides details on how to buy, mix, and measure gluten-free flours for bread; discusses gluten-free bread baking know-how; and presents strategies for making time to bake in your busy life. I have much to tell you and many secrets to share. So go buy some xanthan gum, and let's get baking!

What Can You Expect?

Chances are you didn't grow up watching your mother or grandmother bake gluten-free bread. Even if you grew up baking, gluten-free flours change everything: how you measure ingredients, how much yeast and liquid you use, how you knead, how long the bread rises, and how long it bakes. Although most gluten-free breads are notoriously heavy and dense, they need not be. You *can* make chewy and crusty breads without wheat. But like all things worth achieving in life, you can expect that it will take a little time, thought, and energy.

The recipes in this book have been meticulously fine-tuned to produce excellent results—if you follow the directions. There are almost no shortcuts in baking. Don't bother to try a new baking recipe unless you have the ingredients on hand, the equipment you need, and the time to concentrate and complete the task. I can't tell you how many times I've heard people tell me that a recipe failed and then admit that they substituted ingredients, didn't measure correctly, or were in a rush and probably left a step out.

Read each recipe completely before you actually begin to bake. Follow the directions and measure all ingredients carefully. Baking is the only form of cooking where a little bit too much or too little can ruin a recipe. Save your baking efforts for times when you are prepared. The result will be fabulous breads that you, your family, and your friends will happily consume.

The Science of Baking Bread with Gluten-Free Flours

If you think about how most people bake with wheat, you will realize that they usually use two different kinds of flour: an all-purpose flour for cakes, pies, muffins, and other pastries, and a bread flour for baking bread. The recipes in this book were developed and tested using just one gluten-free flour mix in the Zojirushi® BBCC-X20 Home Bakery Supreme® bread machine.

Few people I know have much time to bake at all, much less have extra time to grab four different flours each time they do. Fewer still have room to store three or four different flour mixes in their cabinets. Following my philosophy that cooking should be simple, I want to be able to reach for a gluten-free bread flour and know it will work dependably for everything I make. The recipes in this book are carefully calibrated to work with my Bread Flour Mix A (see page 6). Be aware that if you do in fact substitute flours, it will probably be necessary to adjust the amounts of other ingredients you use (most likely, the xanthan gum and liquids).

In order to make good gluten-free bread, you will have to set aside all your preconceived notions about how bread should be made. There will be no gluten to hold your bread together and give it the elasticity good bread is known for. You will use xanthan gum to help provide that elasticity and keep it from collapsing. There will be no wheat flavor, but the grainy, nutty flavors of millet and sorghum make delicious sandwich and artisan breads that you will take great delight in eating and serving to others. Finally, there will be no long wait times. There is only one rise, and then the bread starts to bake. You can make a hearty multigrain bread in about two and a half hours.

Gluten-Free Flours for Bread

If you are like me, you have baked and eaten more than your fair share of bad gluten-free bread. Over time, I developed recipes and a flour mix for making some of the breads I missed most. The recipes here were all developed using this one mix as a replacement for wheat bread flour. It will allow you to make breads that taste good, rise evenly, and won't fall when they come out of the bread machine. If you follow the detailed instructions, your gluten-free yeast breads will have the mouth feel and texture of the wheat breads you are familiar with. Moreover, they do not contain rice flour, so they will not have the gummy, glossy look and feel of many of the gluten-free breads you see in stores or of loaves you may have baked in the past.

My bread flour mix is made up of whole-grain flours and starch flours in a 50:50 ratio: it is a combination of millet, sorghum, cornstarch, potato starch (*not* potato flour), and tapioca flour (also called tapioca starch). Millet and sorghum are used to help vary the taste, improve its nutritional value, and provide structure to the dough. The starches help lighten the texture and improve mouth feel.

My Bread Flour Mix A uses more millet than sorghum and has a very slight golden hue. It works well in each of the bread recipes in this book and makes specialty breads that will surpass your wildest expectations. It makes a sandwich bread that is much like homemade wheat bread in terms of its texture and density. The millet and sorghum flour (both whole grain) help keep the loaves fresher than gluten-free breads made of all starchy flours. But remember, real homemade wheat breads never have a shelf life as long as the commercially produced loaves sold in grocery stores today, and neither will your homemade gluten-free bread.

Traditional bread bakers usually use a high-gluten bread flour and then mix it with all-purpose flour, rye flour, or whole-wheat flour in order to alter the taste and texture of their loaves. All of the multi-grain loaves in this book use teff flour, a darker, fiber and protein rich, nutty, and whole-grain flour. Each of the recipes uses a third of a cup of teff flour to replace a third of a cup of bread flour mix. In addition to adding extra nutritional value, teff adds color, texture, and flavor to the bread. You can replace the teff flour with coarsely ground oatmeal (I use a blender to grind it, but you can also use a mortar and pestle), which is my favorite alternate flour to use for multi-grain breads. You may wish to replace it with amaranth, quinoa, or Montina™ if you prefer the much stronger taste of those flours.

I have also created breads that use finely ground nut flour to replace some of the bread flour mix in order to enhance the flavor. Take note: Whenever you add extra whole-grain flour or nut flour, the bread will become slightly denser and heartier. In gluten-free bread baking, less is more, unless you are looking to make a brick.

Make up a large batch of the flour mix so you can bake bread whenever you want by simply reaching into your pantry and grabbing your gluten-free bread flour, just like you might have once reached for wheat bread flour.

Food Philosopher® Gluten-Free Bread Flour Mix
Bread Flour Mix A

⅓ part millet flour	2 cups	1 cup
⅙ part sorghum flour	1 cup	½ cup
⅙ part cornstarch	1 cup	½ cup
⅙ part potato starch	1 cup	½ cup
⅙ part tapioca flour	1 cup	½ cup
Total	6 cups	3 cups

Millet flour, sorghum flour, teff flour, potato starch, tapioca flour, and gluten-free oatmeal can be found in local natural food stores, some grocery stores, and online. The brands seem fairly interchangeable and are consistent in quality. Cornstarch can be found in any grocery store.

How to Measure and Mix Gluten-Free Flours

To measure flour for making flour mixes: Put the empty measuring cup into a small bowl. Use a soup spoon to spoon the flour from the package into the measuring cup, or pour the flour from the package into the measuring cup. Then use a knife or spoon handle to level the top (do this over the bowl to avoid a messy cleanup; pour the flour left in the bowl back into the package or another container). Do not scoop gluten-free flours directly out of the package with the measuring cup.

As each flour is measured, transfer it into a plastic container large enough to leave four or five inches from the top unfilled. Shake container vigorously to mix flours. I usually make 15 cups of Bread Flour Mix A at a time and store and shake it in a 21-cup Rubbermaid® container.

To measure flour for use in recipes: Shake storage container vigorously to mix and aerate the flour mix. Put the empty measuring cup into a small bowl, or hold it over the opening of the container if it is large enough. Use a soup spoon to spoon the flour from the container into the measuring cup, and then use a knife or spoon handle to level the top. If you do this over a bowl, pour the flour left in the bowl back into the storage container. Do not scoop gluten-free flours out of the storage container with the measuring cup. Remember: Shake and bake!

How to Purchase and Store Gluten-Free Flours

Millet, sorghum, and teff flours are whole-grain flours that must be stored carefully. Bread Flour Mix A can be stored at room temperature for about four months. If your house is hot and humid, or if you will not be baking for long periods of time, store the mixes in the refrigerator. Store open packages of millet, sorghum, and teff flour in the refrigerator.

Purchase all these flours from stores or online sellers that have a lot of turnover, so you can be sure you are getting fresh packages. Do not purchase them too far in advance of when you make the flour mixes (more than four months). When you open a new bag, make sure it does not have a strong odor, an indication that it is rancid or old. These flours should have a pleasant grainy and nutty smell. Millet flour in particular tends to get rancid if not stored properly or if it is old (just like whole-wheat flour). Old flours often impart a bitter taste in your baked goods.

Both open and unopened packages of potato starch, tapioca flour, and cornstarch can be stored at room temperature for more than a year. They can be purchased in advance of when you will be using them to make the flour mixes.

The Secrets of Xanthan and Guar Gum

In gluten-free baking, it doesn't matter if you are making cakes, cookies, or bread—xanthan gum is used to replace the gluten in wheat flour. Gluten helps hold baked goods together and gives them elasticity. When using gluten-free flours, you must add back the elasticity by using xanthan gum, or sometimes guar gum. These gums are water soluble; technically, they are called hydrocolloids. Because of their water solubility, xanthan and guar gums improve mouth feel and build viscosity. They help retain moisture, provide elasticity, extend shelf life, encapsulate flavors, and stabilize baked goods so they can be successfully frozen and thawed.

If you use too little xanthan or guar gum, your baked goods will fall apart and/or turn out brittle and hard. If you use too much, your baked goods will condense and shrink after you bake them, growing ever tighter and smaller as the gum works its magic for days after. The amount of xanthan gum needs to be recalibrated for each recipe based on the type and amount of flour mix used; what liquids and flavorings are added (acids exaggerate the effect of the gum); the number of eggs, if any; and the desired texture of the baked good you are trying to make. There is no one-size-fits-all rule for xanthan gum in gluten-free baking. I recommend that you avoid flour mixes that include it as an ingredient.

Xanthan gum is easy to find in natural food stores or online, is fairly consistent in quality across brands, and is very stable over a broad range of temperatures. I recommend it as the gum of choice for every recipe in this book.

The Art of Baking with Gluten-Free Flours

Baking is much more of a science than cooking because the proportions of liquid, flour, salt, sugar, and yeast are so critical to the outcome of the baked good. That said, there is some room for well-planned maneuvering and creativity. Gluten-free baking isn't harder than baking with wheat flour, once you have a good understanding of how gluten-free flours behave, a dependable flour mix, xanthan gum, and a good recipe. In fact, every recipe in this book is based on a good recipe that was originally made with wheat.

Understanding the Essential Nature of Gluten-Free Flours

You probably never considered how much flavor wheat really has until you had to give it up. As a result, you may not realize that one of the things you miss most is the flavor of wheat. In my bread recipes, I try to compensate by using the delicious, nutty-flavored millet and sorghum flours, along with other more transparent flavors, like tapioca flour, cornstarch, and potato starch. The relative transparency of the gluten-free starch-based flours I use allows other flavors to shine through without affecting their taste. You will notice the essence of sesame, pecans, walnuts, and even butter in a whole new light.

Gluten-Free Maneuvering

When I converted these recipes to gluten free, I discovered the amount of liquid in the original wheat-based recipe almost always had to be decreased slightly. I often replaced butter with canola oil, because it tends to produce a lighter gluten-free baked good. I tried to reduce sugar as much as possible, but not enough to negatively impact the bread's taste, moisture, and lightness; and I stayed true to my goal of creating "classic" baked goods versus "sugar free." I also tended to reduce the amount of salt a bit because it stands out against the transparent flours. I increased the amount of yeast.

My all-purpose Bread Flour Mix A can be used in your own treasured family recipes with the kinds of additions and changes noted earlier. You may want to find a recipe in my book that is similar to the one you want to make and see how much xanthan gum, fat, liquid, eggs, and yeast I used. Then, you can start to convert your own recipes using my measurements as a guideline.

Gluten-Free Creativity

You can also use my very dependable recipes as a starting place and make your own changes or additions. Gluten-free bakers have made a number of successful variations to my recipes (eliminating dairy, for example), and I am always grateful when they let me know, so I can encourage others to try. In addition to adding a variety of seeds or finely ground nuts, or replacing a third of a cup of the Bread Flour Mix with another whole-grain flour, such as teff (as noted earlier), you can also add bits of dried fruit or a cheese that is naturally lower in fat (such as Parmesan) to change the nature of the loaves you bake (high-fat cheese gives off too much liquid for use in these recipes and produces a heavy, dense, and undercooked loaf).

Common Questions

Is it possible to use rice, soy, or almond milk? Yes, rice, soy, and almond milks have been successfully used for many of these recipes. Rice and almond milks add less aftertaste, unless you like the taste of soy. Remember that gluten-free flours are rather transparent in flavor.

Is it possible to use sugar alternatives? Sugar acts as a liquid in baking, and since sugar substitutes contain varying amounts of liquid, each recipe would have to be recalibrated for dry/wet proportions and (in some cases) cooking time, depending on which substitute you use. The recipes in this book were originally traditional, classic baked goods made with wheat and granulated sugar. They were not based on recipes for special diets or restricted dietary needs. That said, you could try substituting the sugar alternative of your choice based on your own knowledge of how to make substitutions (for example, rice syrup has been used by some as a sugar substitute in my recipes, but the total amount of several other ingredients had to be adjusted).

How to Measure Ingredients for Recipes in this Book

Measure flour in nesting cups of 1-, ½-, ⅓-, and ¼-cup capacities. Spoon ingredients into the measuring cup and level them off with the edge of a knife or the back of the spoon you used to transfer the ingredients. Measure other dry ingredients in measuring spoons the same way. Take care to be accurate. For instance, as little as an eighth of a teaspoon too much of xanthan gum will affect your baked goods. Measure liquids in glass or plastic measuring cups, and check at eye level.

Invest in an Instant-Read Thermometer

I strongly recommend that you buy an instant-read thermometer, because it will help you make good bread. You will be able to check the temperature of the liquids you use, and when you are trying recipes for the first time, you can use them to check the internal temperature of your breads to make sure they are done (and, if necessary, adjust what you are doing). You do not need a fancy and expensive one: you can find one for less than $5 at your grocery store.

Strategies for Making Time to Bake

Prepare a fresh batch of Bread Flour Mix A whenever you run low, so you'll always have it available. If you have easy access to a pre-mixed flour, you are more likely to bake whenever time is available or the urge strikes. Make sure you have what you need in your baking pantry to make the recipes you want (see pantry recommendations on page 11).

Pre-measure and pre-mix ingredients for breads you know you'll want to make in the course of a month (but remember, do not add the yeast until you are ready to bake). You're more likely to make a loaf of bread if most of the steps have already been completed. Mix and store all the dry ingredients needed for individual breads (except the yeast) in separate, clearly marked containers or tightly sealed plastic bags.

I often try to pre-measure and pre-mix dry ingredients for recipes, so all I have to do is toss in the oil, water (or milk), and eggs (if using) when I am ready to bake. Sometimes, I even pre-measure liquid ingredients and keep them covered (and refrigerated when necessary).

Gluten-Free Bread-Baking Pantry
Non-Refrigerated

- Potato starch (*not* potato flour)
- Tapioca flour (also called tapioca starch)
- Cornstarch
- Sorghum flour (keep refrigerated after opening)
- Millet flour (keep refrigerated after opening)
- Teff flour (keep refrigerated after opening)
- Rye flavoring
- Gluten-free oatmeal
- Xanthan gum
- Granulated sugar
- Dried buttermilk powder (keep refrigerated after opening)
- Canola oil
- Olive oil
- Iodized salt
- A variety of dried herbs and spices, including basil, cardamom, cinnamon, dill weed, fennel seed, oregano, rosemary, sage, and tarragon
- A variety of seeds to use in multi-grain breads, including caraway, poppy, sesame, flax, and sunflower

Refrigerated

- Unsalted butter or margarine
- Eggs (make sure eggs are large and not extra large or medium)

- Milk (I use fat-free for most recipes, but you can use 2%. Do not use whole milk for the recipes in this book; it may create a heavier loaf.)

- Assorted nuts, including walnuts and pecans

The Last Word on Baked Goods

Baked goods are not the largest group recommended for consumption on the Food Guide Pyramid, and they should not make up a significant part of your diet. Try to eat mostly fresh fruits, vegetables, meat, poultry, fish, beans, gluten-free whole grains like quinoa and buckwheat, and low-fat dairy products (but splurge on good cheese if you can!). However, when you do indulge in baked goods, they should be delicious, make you happy, and soothe your longing. Otherwise, why waste the calories?

A recommended source for extra finely ground gluten-free flour:

Authentic Foods®
1860 W. 169th St., Suite B
Gardena, CA 90247
800-806-4737
www.authenticfoods.com

The Art and Science of Using a Bread Machine to Make Gluten-Free Bread

*Bread machines take much of the guesswork out of baking bread. If you start with a dependable, well-crafted recipe, you can be pretty confident that you will be able to slice into a beautiful loaf within two and half hours (plus a little extra time for it to cool). Although it takes longer to bake gluten-free bread in a bread machine than a conventional oven, it requires less effort and hands-on involvement. If you don't plan to toss in any nuts, seeds, or other add-ins during the **KNEAD** cycle, you can basically walk away from it once you turn the machine on (at least until the bread is done and you have to take it out).*

Another benefit: It is relatively easy to figure out what went wrong if your bread fails to rise correctly. The bread machine reduces the number of variables considerably. You put the ingredients into the bread pan, put the pan into the machine, close the top, and press **Start/Restart**—the machine does its work the same basic way every time. If something goes wrong, either the machine was set incorrectly or the ingredients were flawed—or both. Troubleshooting basically comes down to five variables: wrong machine setting, wrong ingredients, ingredients measured incorrectly, ingredients at wrong temperature, or necessary adjustment of the amounts of flour or liquids. It is also important to make sure that the pan is correctly seated in the trough of the bread machine, and make sure that each paddle is squarely placed on its spindle. (There is, of course, also the very slight chance that your machine isn't working correctly.)

The sealed compartment also provides a moist "proofing oven" for the bread during the rise cycle. Moisture is sealed in and can't escape the same way it does when your bread is rising on a counter or in a conventional oven. This is both good and bad. You won't have to worry as much about whether your home is humid or dry (typically a huge variable for bread bakers), but it also means that if you want to bake in a bread machine, bread recipes developed for a stand mixer and conventional oven won't work *as well* as recipes that are developed specifically for a machine: they will require either less liquid or eggs (if specified), or potentially less of both. More importantly, there is a big enough difference among machines that it is best to use gluten-free recipes developed for your particular machine.

Bread Machine Maneuvering

I developed the recipes in this book using the 1-pound-plus loaf recipes from my book *Gluten-Free Baking Classics,* 2nd Edition (Surrey Books, September 2008) as a starting point (all the recipes had originally been based on wheat recipes). I scaled them up to make an almost 2-pound loaf, made sure they worked in a conventional oven, and then adapted them for the bread machine. This usually required reducing liquids, taking out an egg (if applicable), and removing any gelatin (although most of my recipes didn't contain gelatin anyway).

If you have your own favorite 1-pound bread recipes that you want to convert for use in a bread machine, I suggest you start the same way and use my recipes as your guide. If your recipe already makes a 2-pound loaf, start with a similar recipe from this book as a guide to help you make the changes you want or need.

How to Program Your Bread Machine

I used a Zojirushi® BBCC-X20 Home Bakery Supreme® 2-pound Bread Machine to test all the recipes in this book. The majority of my field testers used the Zojirushi BBCC-X20, as well. The X20 and V20 Zojirushi models work the same way, so it doesn't matter which machine you buy. In addition, I asked some of my regular testers who had other machines (Panasonic, Breadman, and Cuisinart) to make the recipes so that I could compare results. Most were able to maneuver their programmable cycles to produce bread of *fairly* comparable taste, texture, and appearance. However, the height of loaves made with these other machines was almost always lower, and there was no uniformity of results among the brands.

The Home Bakery Supreme is designed to produce an oblong traditional sandwich-style loaf. It also permits the home baker to program the time for each of six cycles: **PREHEAT**, **KNEAD**, **RISE 1**, **RISE 2**, **RISE 3**, and **BAKE**. Although I was initially resistant about the idea of bringing a new appliance into my home, I have to admit that the Zojirushi makes a really nice loaf of bread. If you have a Zojirushi, use the settings below. If you have another machine, try to approximate the times listed as closely as possible—although some consideration must also be given to (1) the shape and size of the loaf pan in other machines and (2) the temperature of each cycle (see temperatures for the Home Bakery Supreme on page 16).

For the Home Made – Memory 1 Setting

1. Plug in the Zojirushi bread machine.

2. Press **Select Course** until the arrow points at **HOME MADE – MEMORY 1**.

3. Press **Cycle** until the arrow points at **PREHEAT**. Press **Time** until 10 minutes appears on the screen. Press **Cycle** to lock in the setting.

4. Press **Cycle** until the arrow points at **KNEAD**. Press **Time** until 20 minutes appears on the screen. Press **Cycle** to lock in the setting.

5. Press **Cycle** until the arrow points at **RISE 1**. Press **Time** until OFF appears on the screen. Press **Cycle** to lock in the setting. OFF is the default setting, so if it already says OFF, just press **Cycle**.

6. Press **Cycle** until the arrow points at **RISE 2**. Press **Time** until OFF appears on the screen. Press **Cycle** to lock in the setting. OFF is the default setting, so if it already says OFF, just press **Cycle**.

7. Press **Cycle** until the arrow points at **RISE 3**. Press **Time** until 45 minutes appears on the screen. Press **Cycle** to lock in the setting.

8. Press **Cycle** until the arrow points at **BAKE**. Press **Time** until 70 minutes appears on the screen. Press **Cycle** to lock in the setting.

9. Press **Cycle** until the arrow points at **KEEP WARM**. Press **Time** until OFF appears on the screen. Press **Cycle** to lock in the setting. OFF is the default setting, so if it already says OFF, just press **Cycle**.

According to the Zojirushi BBCC-X20's instruction manual, the machine strives to achieve the following temperatures for each cycle:

- **PREHEAT**: about 82.4°F
- **KNEAD**: remains about constant
- **RISE 1**: about 82.4°F
- **RISE 2**: about 82.4°F
- **RISE 3**: about 100.4°F
- **BAKE**: about 254–290°F
- **KEEP WARM**: about 194°F

Bread-Baking Problems

The most common questions about bread-baking problems include: Why didn't my bread rise? Why didn't my bread rise well? Why did my bread sink in the middle? Why did my bread rise, and then fall?

If you are using a bread machine to make the recipes in this book and you are experiencing these problems, you should ask yourself:

- *Did I program my **HOME MADE – MEMORY 1** setting according to the directions in this book? Did I select the **HOME MADE – MEMORY 1** setting?*

- *Did I check the date on my yeast to make sure it was fresh? The recipes in this book use ¼-ounce packets of active dry yeast granules, which are readily available in grocery stores.*

- *Did I assemble all the ingredients before starting the recipe and make sure all flours, nuts, and seeds were at room temperature?*

- *Were my eggs at room temperature? If not, put them in a bowl of warm water. Make sure your eggs are large and not extra large.*

- *Was my bread machine under the cabinets? Make sure that your machine is not underneath a cabinet or against a wall while bread is baking. Restricting airflow above and around the machine can result in unexpectedly short loaves.*

- *Did I use too much flour?* Too much flour will contribute to a denser, slightly shorter bread. If you think your bread is too dense, try adding 1 less tablespoon of the flour mix the next time you make it.

- *Were all my liquids warmed to between 65°F and 75°F?* If your liquids are below 65°F, your bread may not rise as well as it should. If your liquids are above 75°F, your bread may rise too fast and then sink in the middle when you remove it from the pan, but that's not always true. Sometimes, it's necessary to increase the temperature of the liquids if your bread is well shaped but isn't high enough. See the next section, Critical Insight into How the Zojirushi X20 and V20 Machines Work, for more information.

For bread that sinks or has a crater in the middle:

- *Was I so careful about spooning the flour into the measuring cups that I ended up a little short of flour (either when I made the bread flour mix or when I measured it for the recipe)?* If you think this might be the case, try adding a tablespoon of flour to the dough. If that works, try not to spoon the flour into the cup as lightly the next time you are mixing and measuring flours. The ideal weight for 1 cup of Bread Flour Mix A is between 4.25 and 4.5 ounces. The difference between the two numbers amounts to about 1 tablespoon of the flour mix.

- *Did I measure the liquid correctly?* Too much liquid can cause your bread to fall. If everything else on this list is correct, try reducing the liquid by 1 tablespoon (or 2, if necessary). This might be done instead of or in addition to adding more flour (see the previous bullet).

Critical Insight into How the Zojirushi X20 and V20 Machines Work

Zojirushi bread machines make automatic adjustments in order to get the dough to rise and bake correctly. The **BAKE** cycle temperature self-adjusts depending on the temperature and humidity level in your home and the ingredients in the pan. In other words, it will heat up more for breads with raisins, nuts, and other heavy ingredients; it will heat up more if the temperature in your kitchen is very cool; and it will heat up less if the temperature in your kitchen is very warm. The **BAKE** cycle temperature is typically between the high and low extremes noted earlier in this chapter (254°–290°F).

If the temperature in your kitchen is either very warm or very cool and your bread is well shaped but doesn't rise as high as it should, *and you have made sure that everything else is correct on the list of potential problems*, then the next time you make it, increase the temperature of the liquids to about 85°–90°F to give the yeast more of a boost.

Make sure that your machine is not underneath a cabinet or against a wall while bread is baking. Restricting airflow above and around the machine can result in unexpectedly short loaves.

In addition to the aforementioned self-adjustment the machines make, Zojirushi has found that some slight variation of temperature among machines is to be expected and cannot be controlled. This means that even if two homes' temperature and humidity levels and the bread ingredients are exactly the same, one machine might be baking at 280°F and another might be baking at 272°F. The machine also adjusts for altitude and fluctuations in household current. These differences account for some variations: your bread might not be as fully done as it should be at the end of 70 minutes and might fall a bit, or it might not match the estimated loaf heights I provide for each recipe. There's not much you can do about it, except perhaps adjust the levels of your liquids (most likely, decrease them if your bread is sinking), or adjust the amount of flour you use (see suggestions in the Bread-Baking Problems section on page 16).

Unlike the **BAKE** cycle, which is capable of self-adjusting to a relatively wide range of temperatures, the **RISE 3** cycle tends to hover at about 100.4°F (as noted). However, the **RISE 3** cycle *can* be affected by the same uncontrollable variations in temperature discussed in the preceding paragraph. If you think your bread might simply need more time to rise in order to achieve the ideal height, try allowing it to rise for an additional 10 to 15 minutes by adjusting the **RISE 3** cycle (but remember not to let it rise too long, which can contribute to your loaf falling in the middle).

Breads with Egg and Dairy

Although wheat breads are clearly difficult to reproduce in a gluten-free form, you can still make delicious bread. The recipes in this chapter make tender loaves with the consistency of a homemade white bread and the rich taste of millet and sorghum, two ancient grains that will more than make up for a lack of wheat flavor. They won't harden like a rock or become crumbly if wrapped securely.

These breads are enriched with milk, eggs, and just enough fat to help keep them supple for several days. After that point, they are better served slightly warm (warmed in the toaster, toasted in the toaster, or warmed in the microwave wrapped in a damp paper towel).

This chapter contains many tempting traditional bread recipes for you to try. They are all scaled-up and recalibrated versions of the recipes I use to make bread in a conventional oven. They range from classic Basic and Oatmeal Sandwich Breads to an egg-enriched Challah. I have also included a few special favorites from my own kitchen—Multi-Grain Pecan Sandwich Bread, which makes delicious sandwiches with slices of cold roast chicken or turkey and fresh tomatoes, and the Black Forest Onion–Rye Bread, which makes the best patty melts you've ever eaten. Follow the directions carefully, and you might just find a new favorite or two yourself.

Critical Test Findings

Field testing from around the country for the breads in Chapter 4 provided *slightly* varied results. Breads in this chapter typically rise to anywhere between 3½ to 4¼ inches (and up to 4½ inches if you're lucky or *really* determined). Recommendations follow:

- If your bread is not at least 3½ inches high or falls slightly in the middle, re-read the following sections in Chapter 3: Bread-Baking Problems (page 16) and Critical Insight into How the Zojirushi X20 and V20 Machines Work (page 17).

- Make sure that your machine is not underneath a cabinet or against a wall while bread is baking. Restricting airflow above and around the machine can result in unexpectedly short loaves.

- It is best to remove the bread promptly when it is finished baking; otherwise, it tends to get soft and can fall a bit.

- Whisk the liquids until frothy for the best results.

- Remember to use skim, 1%, or 2% milk for best results. Whole milk seems to create a heavier loaf. Soy and rice milks were also used successfully in field-test kitchens.

- The recipes recommend using a rubber spatula rather than a knife to help release the bread from the bread pan after it has finished baking. Test-kitchen results indicate that *inexpensive* rubber spatulas can melt when pressed against the hot bread pan. Rubbermaid® rubber spatulas worked well, as did several other better-quality brands. You can also use heat-resistant silicone spatulas without any problem.

- These breads should have a nice golden color and should be well shaped. They slice into 16 average-sized slices (more or less, depending on thickness).

Basic Sandwich Bread

Makes 1 loaf

Looking for a delicious sandwich bread? This tender loaf has the consistency of a homemade white bread, and it won't harden like a rock or become crumbly. This bread is perfect for making kid-friendly peanut-butter-and-jelly sandwiches for a school lunch or scrumptious grilled cheese or Philly cheesesteak sandwiches if you're near a stove. It's also terrific for making buttered toast.

1¼ cups skim, 1%, or 2% milk (between 65°F and 75°F)

¼ cup canola oil (between 65°F and 75°F)

2 large eggs (room temperature)

3 cups Bread Flour Mix A (see page 6)

3 tablespoons sugar

2¼ teaspoons xanthan gum

¾ teaspoon salt

1 packet (¼ ounce) active dry yeast granules (not quick-rise)

1. Set your Zojirushi bread machine to **HOME MADE – MEMORY 1** (see page 15). Press **Crust Control** until the arrow points to Medium.

2. Remove bread pan from machine and make sure kneading blades are firmly secured in place.

3. Whisk milk, canola oil, and eggs together until frothy (bubbles at the top) in a glass measuring cup and pour into the bread pan.

4. Whisk Bread Flour Mix A, sugar, xanthan

Cook's Notes:

Dry ingredients can be pre-mixed ahead of time and stored in plastic containers for future use. However, do not add yeast until you are just about to bake bread.

Ideally, this bread should be about 4 to 4¼ inches high in the very center of the loaf. The height of your bread may vary slightly. Refer to page 21 for more information.

gum, salt, and yeast in a small mixing bowl or container until well combined and sprinkle over the liquids. Without pressing down excessively hard, try to spread out the dry ingredients so they cover all the liquid.

5. Put the bread pan into the machine, secure it in place, and close the lid. Press **Start/Restart**.

6. Optional, but suggested: During **KNEAD** cycle, scrape the pan with a rubber spatula if flour clings to sides.

7. Remove bread pan from machine promptly when the **BAKE** cycle ends. Turn bread pan over to remove bread and place it on a rack to cool (use a rubber spatula to release it if it sticks, so you don't scrape the nonstick pan). Bread should have a hollow sound when you tap on bottom and sides. Instant-read thermometer should register about 205°F. Store in refrigerator for up to 1 week or freezer for up to 3 weeks. Can be cut into 16 slices, not including ends.

Buttermilk Sandwich Bread

Old-fashioned buttermilk bread makes a great sandwich or a golden piece of toast. The buttermilk helps to keep the bread softer and more tender (i.e., fresher) than traditional loaves made with regular milk.

1. Prepare Basic Sandwich Bread recipe according to instructions, except substitute 1 cup plus 3

Cook's Note:
Ideally, this bread should be about 4 inches high in the very center of the loaf. The height of your bread may vary slightly. Refer to page 21 for more information.

tablespoons fresh buttermilk (between 65°F and 75°F) or 1 cup plus 3 tablespoons water (between 65°F and 75°F) and 5 tablespoons buttermilk powder for regular milk in recipe.

Irish Soda Yeast Sandwich Bread

If you love the taste of Irish Soda Bread, this bread could become a favorite. I've combined raisins, caraway seeds, and buttermilk to create a tender loaf reminiscent of the original version, which featured baking soda.

Cook's Note:
Ideally, this bread should be about 4 inches high in the very center of the loaf. The height of your bread may vary slightly. Refer to page 21 for more information.

1. Prepare Basic Sandwich Bread recipe according to instructions, except substitute 1 cup plus 3 tablespoons fresh buttermilk (between 65°F and 75°F) or 1 cup plus 3 tablespoons water (between 65°F and 75°F) and 5 tablespoons buttermilk powder for regular milk in recipe.

2. During **KNEAD** cycle: add ¾ to 1 cup raisins and 1½ tablespoons caraway seeds when machine beeps and the ADD indicator flashes. Scrape the pan with a rubber spatula if flour and/or seeds cling to the sides.

Oatmeal Sandwich Bread

Makes 1 loaf

Ground oatmeal lends a touch of chewiness to this flavorful bread. It makes delicious sandwiches, including grilled cheese and paninis. Toss in some sesame seeds while it kneads in order to add a little complexity and variety to the bread (recipe follows). This is a great everyday loaf for kids big and small.

1 cup plus 2 tablespoons skim, 1%, or 2% milk
   (between 65°F and 75°F)

¼ cup canola oil (between 65°F and 75°F)

2 large eggs (room temperature)

2⅔ cups Bread Flour Mix A (see page 6)

⅓ cup coarsely ground oatmeal

3 tablespoons sugar

2¼ teaspoons xanthan gum

¾ teaspoon salt

1 packet (¼ ounce) active dry yeast granules (not quick-rise)

1. Set your Zojirushi bread machine to **HOME MADE – MEMORY 1** (see page 15). Press **Crust Control** until the arrow points to Medium.

2. Remove bread pan from machine and make sure kneading blades are firmly secured in place.

3. Whisk milk, canola oil, and eggs together until frothy (bubbles at the top) in a glass measuring cup and pour into the bread pan.

Cook's Notes:
Dry ingredients can be pre-mixed ahead of time and stored in plastic containers for future use. However, do not add yeast until you are just about to bake bread.

Ideally, this bread should be about 3½ to 3¾ inches high in the very center of the loaf. The height of your bread may vary slightly. Refer to page 21 for more information.

4. Whisk Bread Flour Mix A, oatmeal, sugar, xanthan gum, salt, and yeast in a small mixing bowl or container until well combined and sprinkle over the liquids. Without pressing down excessively hard, try to spread out the dry ingredients so they cover all the liquid.

5. Put the bread pan into the machine, secure it in place, and close the lid. Press **Start/Restart**.

6. Optional, but suggested: During **KNEAD** cycle, scrape the pan with a rubber spatula if flour clings to sides.

7. Remove bread pan from machine promptly when the **BAKE** cycle ends. Turn bread pan over to remove bread and place it on a rack to cool (use a rubber spatula to release the bread if it sticks, so you won't scrape the nonstick pan). Bread should have a hollow sound when you tap on bottom and sides. Instant-read thermometer should register about 205°F. Store in refrigerator for up to 1 week or freezer for up to 3 weeks. Can be cut into 16 slices, not including ends.

Oatmeal–Sesame Sandwich Bread

1. During **KNEAD** cycle: add 2½ to 3 tablespoons sesame seeds when machine beeps and the ADD indicator flashes. Scrape the pan with a rubber spatula if flour or seeds cling to the sides.

Rye Sandwich Bread

Makes 1 loaf

How do you make rye bread without rye flour, which has gluten? The trick is to use teff flour to provide the hearty richness and color this bread is known for. A touch of rye flavoring, which is now available in a gluten-free form, provides the necessary finishing touch. Rye bread is delicious and makes incredible grilled cheese sandwiches, patty melts and—when you're in the mood for something different—savory bread crumbs for chicken cutlets that are extra delicious when topped with a bit of Gruyère cheese.

1 cup plus 3 tablespoons skim, 1%, or 2% milk (between 65°F and 75°F)

¼ cup canola oil (between 65°F and 75°F)

2 large eggs (room temperature)

2⅔ cups Bread Flour Mix A (see page 6)

⅓ cup teff flour

3 tablespoons sugar

2¼ teaspoons xanthan gum

¾ teaspoon salt

1½ teaspoons rye flavor*

1 packet (¼ ounce) active dry yeast granules (not quick-rise)

2½–3 tablespoons caraway seeds (or to taste)

1. Set your Zojirushi bread machine to **HOME MADE – MEMORY 1** (see page 15). Press **Crust Control** until the arrow points to Medium.

Cook's Notes:

Dry ingredients can be pre-mixed ahead of time and stored in plastic containers for future use. However, do not add yeast until you are just about to bake bread.

Ideally, this bread should be about 4 inches high in the very center of the loaf. The height of your bread may vary slightly. Refer to page 21 for more information.

This bread has a classic New York deli–style rye taste. After you make it the first time, you can adjust the amount of rye flavor according to your preference. If you prefer it milder, decrease it in ½-teaspoon increments. For a stronger rye flavor, increase it in ½-teaspoon increments.

* An excellent gluten-free rye flavor is available from Authentic Foods (see page 12 for details).

---

2. Remove bread pan from machine and make sure kneading blades are firmly secured in place.

3. Whisk milk, canola oil, and eggs together until frothy (bubbles at the top) in a glass measuring cup and pour into the bread pan.

4. Whisk Bread Flour Mix A, teff flour, sugar, xanthan gum, salt, rye flavor, and yeast in a small mixing bowl or container until well combined and sprinkle over the liquids. Without pressing down excessively hard, try to spread out the dry ingredients so they cover all the liquid.

5. Put the bread pan into the machine, secure it in place, and close the lid. Press **Start/Restart**.

6. During **KNEAD** cycle: add 2½ to 3 tablespoons caraway seeds when machine beeps and the ADD indicator flashes. Scrape the pan with a rubber spatula if flour and/or seeds cling to the sides.

7. Remove bread pan from machine promptly when the **BAKE** cycle ends. Turn bread pan over to remove bread and place it on a rack to cool (use a rubber spatula to release the bread if it sticks, so you won't scrape the nonstick pan). Bread should have a hollow sound when you tap on bottom and sides. Instant-read thermometer should register about 205°F. Store in refrigerator for up to 1 week or freezer for up to 3 weeks. Can be cut into 16 slices, not including ends.

Black Forest Onion–Rye Sandwich Bread

My grandmother came from the Black Forest region of Germany, and this bread, which is also called Zweibelbrot, reminds me of her. It makes nice moist slices for a delicious sandwich and goes well alongside sausages, wursts, cheeses, and mustards.

1. Melt 1 tablespoon butter in a medium-sized frying pan over medium heat. Stir in 1 cup finely diced onion and cook until softened, but not browned. Put onions in a small dish and set aside to cool. Make sure mixture is not too wet.

2. During **KNEAD** cycle: add cooked onions (in addition to the 2½ to 3 tablespoons of caraway seeds) when machine beeps and the ADD indicator flashes. Scrape the pan with a rubber spatula if flour, onions, and/or seeds cling to the sides.

Pecan Sandwich Bread

Makes 1 loaf

Pecans add a touch of sweetness to this hearty, versatile loaf. I use finely ground pecans to enrich the dough and chopped pecans to add texture and flavor. Slices of this bread are delicious with your favorite nut butters and fruit preserves, and it makes a great sandwich, especially with roast turkey or chicken and slices of fresh tomato. The Pecan–Raisin version (recipe follows) is a great bread to serve with soup and salads. It's sure to become a favorite.

1 cup plus 2 tablespoons skim, 1%, or 2% milk (between 65°F and 75°F)

¼ cup canola oil (between 65°F and 75°F)

2 large eggs (room temperature)

2⅔ cups Bread Flour Mix A (see page 6)

⅓ cup finely ground pecans

3 tablespoons sugar

2¼ teaspoons xanthan gum

¾ teaspoon salt

1 packet (¼ ounce) active dry yeast granules (not quick-rise)

¾ cup chopped pecans

1. Set your Zojirushi bread machine to **HOME MADE – MEMORY 1** (see page 15). Press **Crust Control** until the arrow points to Medium.

2. Remove bread pan from machine and make sure kneading blades are firmly secured in place.

3. Whisk milk, canola oil, and eggs together until

Cook's Notes:
Dry ingredients can be pre-mixed ahead of time and stored in plastic containers for future use. However, do not add yeast until you are just about to bake bread.

Ideally, this bread should be about 3½ to 4 inches high in the very center of the loaf. The height of your bread may vary slightly. Refer to page 21 for more information.

frothy (bubbles at the top) in a glass measuring cup and pour into the bread pan.

4. Whisk Bread Flour Mix A, finely ground pecans, sugar, xanthan gum, salt, and yeast in a small mixing bowl or container until well combined and sprinkle over the liquids. Without pressing down excessively hard, try to spread out the dry ingredients so they cover all the liquid.

5. Put the bread pan into the machine, secure it in place, and close the lid. Press **Start/Restart**.

6. During **KNEAD** cycle: add ¾ cup chopped pecans when machine beeps and the ADD indicator flashes. Scrape the pan with a rubber spatula if flour and/or nuts cling to the sides.

7. Remove bread pan from machine promptly when the **BAKE** cycle ends. Turn bread pan over to remove bread and place it on a rack to cool (use a rubber spatula to release the bread if it sticks, so you won't scrape the nonstick pan). Bread should have a hollow sound when you tap on bottom and sides. Instant-read thermometer should register about 205°F. Store in refrigerator for up to 1 week or freezer for up to 3 weeks. Can be cut into 16 slices, not including ends.

Pecan–Raisin Sandwich Bread

1. During **KNEAD** cycle: add ⅔ cup raisins (in addition to ⅔ cup chopped pecans) when machine beeps and the ADD indicator flashes. Scrape the pan with a rubber spatula if flour, raisins, or nuts cling to the sides.

Cook's Notes:

Dry ingredients can be pre-mixed ahead of time and stored in plastic containers for future use. However, do not add yeast until you are just about to bake bread.

Ideally, this bread should be about 3½ to 4 inches high in the very center of the loaf. The height of your bread may vary slightly. Refer to page 21 for more information.

Walnut Sandwich Bread

Makes 1 loaf

Walnuts give this fragrant bread an intriguing character and depth. You can enjoy it for breakfast, topped with fruit preserves and nut butter, or for lunch alongside soup and a salad. I like to serve the Walnut–Raisin Sandwich Bread (recipe follows) with cheese, and the Cranberry–Walnut version (recipe follows) makes a great sandwich with roast turkey or chicken.

1 cup plus 2 tablespoons skim, 1%, or 2% milk (between 65°F and 75°F)

¼ cup canola oil (between 65°F and 75°F)

2 large eggs (room temperature)

2⅔ cups Bread Flour Mix A (see page 6)

⅓ cup finely ground walnuts

3 tablespoons sugar

2¼ teaspoons xanthan gum

¾ teaspoon salt

1 packet (¼ ounce) active dry yeast granules (not quick-rise)

¾ cup chopped walnuts

1. Set your Zojirushi bread machine to **HOME MADE – MEMORY 1** (see page 15). Press **Crust Control** until the arrow points to Medium.

2. Remove bread pan from machine and make sure kneading blades are firmly secured in place.

3. Whisk milk, canola oil, and eggs together until frothy (bubbles at the top) in a glass measuring cup and pour into the bread pan.

4. Whisk Bread Flour Mix A, finely ground walnuts, sugar, xanthan gum, salt, and yeast in a small mixing bowl or container until well combined and sprinkle over the liquids. Without pressing down excessively hard, try to spread out the dry ingredients so they cover all the liquid.

5. Put the bread pan into the machine, secure it in place, and close the lid. Press **Start/Restart**.

6. During **KNEAD** cycle: add ¾ cup chopped walnuts when machine beeps and the ADD indicator flashes. Scrape the pan with a rubber spatula if flour and/or nuts cling to the sides.

7. Remove bread pan from machine promptly when the **BAKE** cycle ends. Turn bread pan over to remove bread and place it on a rack to cool (use a rubber spatula to release the bread if it sticks, so you won't scrape the nonstick pan). Bread should have a hollow sound when you tap on bottom and sides. Instant-read thermometer should register about 205°F. Store in refrigerator for up to 1 week or freezer for up to 3 weeks. Can be cut into 16 slices, not including ends.

Walnut–Raisin Sandwich Bread

1. During **KNEAD** cycle: add ⅔ cup raisins (in addition to ⅔ cup chopped walnuts) when machine beeps and the ADD indicator flashes. Scrape the pan with a rubber spatula if flour, raisins, or nuts cling to the sides.

Cranberry–Walnut Yeast Sandwich Bread

1. During **KNEAD** cycle: add ⅔ cup dried cranberries (in addition to ⅔ cup chopped walnuts) when machine beeps and the ADD indicator flashes. Scrape the pan with a rubber spatula if flour, cranberries, and/or nuts cling to the sides.

Multi-Grain Sandwich Bread

Makes 1 loaf

You can bake a rich variety of multi-grain gluten-free sandwich breads simply by substituting a third of a cup of whole-grain flour for a third of a cup of the Bread Flour Mix A. I really like teff flour, which makes a delicious, hearty bread reminiscent of a whole-wheat loaf, but you could substitute amaranth, quinoa, or Montina if you prefer. I like to add sesame seeds, sunflower seeds, and golden flax seeds, but you can add your own favorites in whatever proportions you want (but don't add more than 6 tablespoons total, or your bread will be too dense). The nut versions (recipes follow) are also delicious and make great sandwiches.

Cook's Notes:
Dry ingredients can be pre-mixed ahead of time and stored in plastic containers for future use. However, do not add yeast until you are just about to bake bread.

Ideally, this bread should be about 3½ to 3¾ inches high in the very center of the loaf. The height of your bread may vary slightly. Refer to page 21 for more information.

1 cup plus 3 tablespoons skim, 1%, or 2% milk (between 65°F and 75°F)

¼ cup canola oil (between 65°F and 75°F)

2 large eggs (room temperature)

2⅔ cups Bread Flour Mix A (see page 6)

⅓ cup teff flour

3 tablespoons sugar

2¼ teaspoons xanthan gum

¾ teaspoon salt

1 packet (¼ ounce) active dry yeast granules (not quick-rise)

2 tablespoons sesame seeds

2 tablespoons flax seeds

2 tablespoons sunflower seeds

1. Set your Zojirushi bread machine to **HOME MADE – MEMORY 1** (see page 15). Press **Crust Control** until the arrow points to Medium.

2. Remove bread pan from machine and make sure kneading blades are firmly secured in place.

3. Whisk milk, canola oil, and eggs together until frothy (bubbles at the top) in a glass measuring cup and pour into the bread pan.

4. Whisk Bread Flour Mix A, teff flour, sugar, xanthan gum, salt, and yeast in a small mixing bowl or container until well combined and sprinkle over the liquids. Without pressing down excessively hard, try to spread out the dry ingredients so they cover all the liquid.

5. Put the bread pan into the machine, secure it in place, and close the lid. Press **Start/Restart**.

6. During **KNEAD** cycle: add sesame, flax, and sunflower seeds when machine beeps and the ADD indicator flashes. Scrape the pan with a rubber spatula if flour and/or seeds cling to the sides.

7. Remove bread pan from machine promptly when the **BAKE** cycle ends. Turn bread pan over to remove bread and place it on a rack to cool (use a rubber spatula to release the bread if it sticks, so you won't scrape the nonstick pan). Bread should have a hollow sound when you tap on bottom and sides. Instant-read thermometer should register about 205°F. Store in refrigerator for up to 1 week or freezer for up to 3 weeks. Can be cut into 16 slices, not including ends.

Multi-Grain Pecan Sandwich Bread

1. During **KNEAD** cycle: add ¾ cup chopped pecans (and up to 2 tablespoons seeds, if desired) when machine beeps and the ADD indicator flashes. Scrape the pan with a rubber spatula if flour and/or nuts cling to the sides.

Multi-Grain Walnut Sandwich Bread

1. During **KNEAD** cycle: add ¾ cup chopped walnuts (and up to 2 tablespoons seeds, if desired) when machine beeps and the ADD indicator flashes. Scrape the pan with a rubber spatula if flour and/or nuts cling to the sides.

Cinnamon Swirl Bread

Makes 1 loaf

Wake up to the warm scent of cinnamon toast floating through the air. In order to make cinnamon bread, wheat bakers typically roll bread dough into a large rectangle, sprinkle cinnamon sugar over it, and then roll it into a log before putting it into a loaf pan. Gluten-free bread dough is too soft to roll, unfortunately, and if you want to make this swirl loaf in a bread machine, you'll need confidence and a sure hand with a spatula. The end result is worth the effort: a golden loaf bursting with cinnamon flavor and topped with a touch of cinnamon sugar. Try it and you'll see. The leftover bread makes great French toast or bread pudding. The Cinnamon–Raisin version (recipe follows) makes incredible toast for breakfast.

> ½ cup granulated sugar
>
> 2 teaspoons cinnamon
>
> 1 cup plus 3 tablespoons skim, 1%, or 2% milk (between 65°F and 75°F)
>
> 3 tablespoons canola oil (between 65°F and 75°F)
>
> 2 large eggs (room temperature)
>
> 3 cups Bread Flour Mix A (see page 6)
>
> 3 tablespoons sugar
>
> 2¼ teaspoons xanthan gum
>
> ¾ teaspoon salt
>
> 1 packet (¼ ounce) active dry yeast granules (not quick-rise)

1. Set your Zojirushi bread machine to **HOME MADE – MEMORY 1** (see page 15). Press **Crust Control** until the arrow points to Medium.

Cook's Notes:
Dry ingredients can be pre-mixed ahead of time and stored in plastic containers for future use. However, do not add yeast until you are just about to bake bread.

Ideally, this bread should be about 3½ to 4 inches high in the very center of the loaf. The height of your bread may vary slightly. Refer to page 21 for more information.

2. Remove bread pan from machine and make sure kneading blades are firmly secured in place.

3. Combine ½ cup granulated sugar and 2 teaspoons cinnamon in a small bowl and set aside.

4. Whisk milk, canola oil, and eggs together until frothy (bubbles at the top) in a glass measuring cup and pour into the bread pan.

5. Whisk Bread Flour Mix A, sugar, xanthan gum, salt, and yeast in a small mixing bowl or container until well combined and sprinkle over the liquids. Without pressing down excessively hard, try to spread out the dry ingredients so they cover all the liquid.

6. Put the bread pan into the machine, secure it in place, and close the lid. Press **Start/Restart**.

7. Optional, but suggested: During **KNEAD** cycle, scrape the pan with a rubber spatula if flour clings to sides.

8. When the timer reads 1:55 and the machine stops kneading, quickly sprinkle all the cinnamon sugar *except 1 tablespoon* down the center of the dough. Use a rubber spatula to fold the cinnamon sugar into the bread (about 6 to 8 turns), making sure there isn't any sugar sitting in a tiny pile at the bottom of the bread pan. Smooth out the top of the bread. Sprinkle remaining 1 tablespoon of cinnamon sugar across the top of the bread.

9. Remove bread pan from machine promptly when the **BAKE** cycle ends. Turn bread pan over to remove bread and place it on a rack to cool (use a rubber spatula to release the bread if it sticks, so you won't scrape the nonstick pan). Bread should have a hollow sound when you tap on bottom and sides. Instant-read thermometer should register about 205°F. Store in refrigerator for up to 1 week or freezer for up to 3 weeks. Can be cut into 16 slices, not including ends.

Cinnamon–Raisin Bread

1. During **KNEAD** cycle: add ¾ to 1 cup raisins when machine beeps and the ADD indicator flashes. Scrape the pan with a rubber spatula if flour and/or raisins cling to the sides. After the **KNEAD** cycle is complete, proceed with steps 8 and 9 of the Cinnamon Swirl Bread recipe.

Challah Bread

Makes 1 loaf

Homemade gluten-free challah does not have the squishy feel of commercially made challahs prepared with highly refined wheat flour. The recipe below makes a bread that will be more like the homemade traditional challah I found recipes for in turn-of-the-century cookbooks (my favorite is The Settlement Cook Book: The Way to a Man's Heart *by Mrs. Simon Kander). If you truly crave an egg-glazed top, you can quickly brush some beaten egg (not too much!) on the top of the dough immediately after the knead cycle stops (see step 7 in the recipe instructions). However, don't attempt this until you've already prepared the recipe once and are familiar with how the recipe normally turns out. Try the version with raisins for the holidays.*

Cook's Notes:
Dry ingredients can be pre-mixed ahead of time and stored in plastic containers for future use. However, do not add yeast until you are just about to bake bread.

Ideally, this bread should be about 3¾ to 4½ inches high in the very center of the loaf. The height of your bread may vary slightly. Refer to page 21 for more information.

1 cup water (between 65°F and 75°F)

2 teaspoons canola oil (between 65°F and 75°F)

3 large eggs (room temperature)

3 cups Bread Flour Mix A (see page 6)

3 tablespoons granulated sugar

2¼ teaspoons xanthan gum

¾ teaspoon salt

1 packet (¼ ounce) active dry yeast granules (not quick-rise)

1 tablespoon sesame or poppy seeds for top of bread, optional

1. Set your Zojirushi bread machine to **HOME MADE – MEMORY 1** (see page 15). Press **Crust Control** until the arrow points to Medium.

2. Remove bread pan from machine and make sure kneading blades are firmly secured in place.

3. Whisk water, canola oil, and eggs together until very frothy (lots of bubbles at the top) in a glass measuring cup and pour into the bread pan.

4. Whisk Bread Flour Mix A, sugar, xanthan gum, salt, and yeast in a small mixing bowl or container until well combined and sprinkle over the liquids. Without pressing down excessively hard, try to spread out the dry ingredients so they cover all the liquid.

5. Put the bread pan into the machine, secure it in place, and close the lid. Press **Start/Restart**.

6. Optional, but suggested: During **KNEAD** cycle, scrape the pan with a rubber spatula if flour clings to sides.

7. Optional: When the timer reads 1:55 and the machine stops kneading, quickly use an offset spatula or butter knife to smooth the top of the dough. Starting at the upper left-hand corner of the loaf, use a very sharp, pointed knife to draw a large repetitive "S" pattern down the middle of the loaf, from one end to the other. Next, start from the opposite corner and repeat the process. When you are finished, you will have drawn a braid on top of the dough. (If a glazed appearance is desired, at this point you should *very quickly* brush the top of the dough with a well-beaten egg, but it is imperative that this is done *very quickly*.) Sprinkle 1 tablespoon sesame or poppy seeds across top of dough, if desired.

8. Remove bread pan from machine promptly when the **BAKE** cycle ends. Turn bread pan over to remove bread and place it on a rack to cool (use a rubber spatula to release the bread if it sticks, so you won't scrape the nonstick pan). Bread should have a hollow sound when you tap on bottom and sides. Instant-read thermometer should register about 205°F. Store in refrigerator for up to 1 week or freezer for up to 3 weeks. Can be cut into 16 slices, not including ends.

Challah Bread with Raisins

1. During **KNEAD** cycle: add ¾ to 1 cup raisins when machine beeps and the ADD indicator flashes. Scrape the pan with a rubber spatula if flour and/or raisins cling to the sides.

Babka (Ukrainian Style)

Makes 1 loaf

Cook's Notes:
Dry ingredients can be pre-mixed ahead of time and stored in plastic containers for future use. However, do not add yeast until you are just about to bake bread.

Ideally, this bread should be about 3¾ to 4½ inches high in the very center of the loaf. The height of your bread may vary slightly. Refer to page 21 for more information.

We always looked forward to Ukrainian Easter when I was young, because that's when we'd receive a coveted Babka from John and Mary Fizer's kitchen. The Fizers always made so many Babkas for the holiday that they baked some of them in coffee cans. The unique shape was only part of the charm; the egg-enriched, sweetened bread we loved to eat was also studded with rum-infused golden raisins. This bread-machine version is delicious served with fresh, creamy butter and fruit preserves for breakfast or brunch. Cut thick slices after it cools or toast it lightly for several days after.

1 cup golden raisins

2 teaspoons rum

1 cup skim, 1%, or 2% milk (between 65°F and 75°F)

2 tablespoons unsalted butter, melted and cooled to between 65°F and 75°F

3 large eggs (room temperature)

3 cups Bread Flour Mix A (see page 6)

⅓ cup granulated sugar

2¼ teaspoons xanthan gum

¾ teaspoon salt

1 packet (¼ ounce) active dry yeast granules (not quick-rise)

1. Set your Zojirushi bread machine to **HOME MADE – MEMORY 1** (see page 15). Press **Crust Control** until the arrow points to Medium.

2. Remove bread pan from machine and make sure kneading blades are firmly secured in place.

3. Combine 1 cup golden raisins and 2 teaspoons rum in a small bowl and set aside.

4. Whisk milk, melted butter, and eggs together until frothy (bubbles at the top) in a glass measuring cup and pour into the bread pan.

5. Whisk Bread Flour Mix A, sugar, xanthan gum, salt, and yeast in a small mixing bowl or container until well combined and sprinkle over the liquids. Without pressing down excessively hard, try to spread out the dry ingredients so they cover all the liquid.

6. Put the bread pan into the machine, secure it in place, and close the lid. Press **Start/Restart**.

7. During **KNEAD** cycle: add 1 cup raisins when machine beeps and the ADD indicator flashes. Scrape the pan with a rubber spatula if flour and/or raisins cling to the sides.

8. Remove bread pan from machine promptly when the **BAKE** cycle ends. Turn bread pan over to remove bread and place it on a rack to cool (use a rubber spatula to release the bread if it sticks, so you won't scrape the nonstick pan). Bread should have a hollow sound when you tap on bottom and sides. Instant-read thermometer should register about 205°F. Store in refrigerator for up to 1 week or freezer for up to 3 weeks. Can be cut into 16 slices, not including ends.

Holiday Breakfast Bread

You may choose to follow the suggestion for add-ins described in Step 1 below, or make this slightly sweet egg bread with any combination of dried or candied fruit that suits your family traditions.

1. Omit raisins and rum in the Babka recipe and substitute 1 cup chopped assorted candied fruit *or* ½ cup candied orange peel (or citron) and ½ cup golden raisins.

2. Optional: When the timer says 1:55 and the machine stops kneading, quickly sprinkle 1 tablespoon granulated sugar over top of bread.

Other suggestions for the Holiday Breakfast Bread:

*   Add 1 teaspoon ground cinnamon *or* ½ to ¾ teaspoon ground cardamom to the Babka recipe's Step 5, if desired.

*   Or add 1 teaspoon pure almond extract to the Babka recipe's Step 4.

*   Or add up to 1 tablespoon grated lemon or orange rind to the Babka recipe's Step 5.

Breads without Egg and Dairy

The breads in this chapter all started out as crusty, chewy artisan loaves baked in a French-bread pan in a conventional oven (see Gluten-Free Baking Classics, 2nd Edition, Surrey Books, 2008). *I used my own recipes as the starting point.*

FRENCH–ITALIAN SANDWICH BREAD

Panini Sandwich Bread

Onion–Dill Sandwich Bread

Rosemary–Olive Sandwich Bread

Sun-Dried Tomato and Roasted Garlic Sandwich Bread

Parmesan Sandwich Bread*

OATMEAL ARTISAN BREAD

Oatmeal–Sesame Artisan Bread

RYE ARTISAN BREAD

Black Forest Onion–Rye Artisan Bread

Swedish Rye Artisan Bread

PECAN ARTISAN BREAD

Pecan–Raisin Artisan Bread

WALNUT ARTISAN BREAD

Walnut–Raisin Artisan Bread

Cranberry–Walnut Yeast Artisan Bread

MULTI-GRAIN ARTISAN BREAD

Multi-Grain Pecan Artisan Bread

Multi-Grain Walnut Artisan Bread

GOLDEN ITALIAN ARTISAN BREAD WITH RAISINS AND FENNEL

* Contains added dairy in the form of cheese

None of the original recipes contained egg or dairy, and they all made delicious-tasting loaves that came closer to the texture and appearance of artisan wheat breads than any other recipes I've ever found. Naturally, they lacked wheat flavor, but the nutty, grainy flavor of millet and sorghum more than made up for it. Unfortunately, the bread machine cannot create the thick, crunchy crusts I personally long for in an artisan bread, but it does make an excellent, chewy bread with a lovely (albeit a bit pale) crust. These breads are slightly firmer than those in Chapter 4, and they do not stay as supple several days after you bake them because they contain significantly less fat to keep them soft. (They contain less oil overall and no eggs or milk.)

These breads are excellent to serve fresh alongside a meal—particularly a stew, soup, or salad. They make really good sandwiches, especially within the first two days. They also make great toast, crostini, grilled cheese, and panini. After the second day, most (but not all) testers found the bread to be softer if it was served slightly warm rather than cold (warmed in the toaster, toasted in the toaster, or warmed in the microwave wrapped in a damp paper towel). One resourceful tester sent her son to school with an already cooked and cooled panini every day because she found it to be the best way to maintain the integrity of the bread.

No matter how *you* choose to eat these breads, you will find them a welcome addition to your baking repertoire.

Critical Test Findings

Field testing from around the country for the breads in Chapter 5 provided *slightly* varied results. Breads in this chapter typically rise to anywhere between 3 to 3¾ inches (and up to 4 inches, if you're lucky or *really* determined). Recommendations follow:

- If your bread is not at least 3 inches high or falls slightly in the middle, re-read the following sections in Chapter 3: Bread-Baking Problems (page 16) and Critical Insight into How the Zojirushi X20 and V20 Machines Work (page 17).

- Make sure that your machine is not underneath a cabinet or against a wall while bread is baking. Restricting airflow above and around the machine can result in unexpectedly short loaves.

- The recipes recommend using a rubber spatula rather than a knife to help release the bread from the bread pan after it has finished baking. Test-kitchen results indicate that *inexpensive* rubber spatulas can melt when pressed against the hot bread pan. Rubbermaid® rubber spatulas worked well, as did several other better-quality brands. You can also use heat-resistant silicone spatulas without any problem.

- These breads should have a nice golden color on the sides and a pale top crust. They are generally well shaped and slice into 16 average-sized slices (more or less, depending on thickness).

French–Italian Sandwich Bread

Makes 1 loaf

Cook's Notes:
Dry ingredients can be pre-mixed ahead of time and stored in plastic containers for future use. However, do not add yeast until you are just about to bake bread.

Ideally, this bread should be about 3½ to 3¾ inches high in the very center of the loaf. The height of your bread may vary slightly. Refer to page 49 for more information.

Although it started out as a crusty, baguette-shaped loaf, this bread-machine French–Italian Sandwich Bread has a paler, softer crust, but it retains the same fragrant, grainy taste and chewy texture of the original. It makes delicious sandwiches, grilled cheese, and panini and will work well alongside any meal you serve.

1½ cups water (between 65°F and 75°F)

2 teaspoons olive oil (between 65°F and 75°F)

3 cups Bread Flour Mix A (see page 6)

3 tablespoons sugar

2 teaspoons xanthan gum

1 teaspoon salt

1 packet (¼ ounce) active dry yeast granules (not quick-rise)

1. Set Zojirushi Bread Machine to **HOME MADE – MEMORY 1** (see page 15). Press **Crust Control** until the arrow points to Dark.

2. Remove bread pan from machine and make sure kneading blades are firmly secured in place.

3. Whisk water and olive oil in a glass measuring cup and pour into the bread pan.

4. Whisk Bread Flour Mix A, sugar, xanthan gum, salt, and yeast in a small mixing bowl or container until well combined and sprinkle over the liquids. Without pressing down excessively hard, try to spread out the dry ingredients so they cover all the liquid.

5. Put the bread pan into the machine, secure it in place, and close the lid. Press **Start/Restart**.

6. Optional, but suggested: During **KNEAD** cycle, scrape the pan with a rubber spatula if flour clings to sides.

7. Remove bread pan from machine promptly when the **BAKE** cycle ends. Turn bread pan over to remove bread and place it on a rack to cool (use a rubber spatula to release the bread if it sticks, so you won't scrape the nonstick pan). Bread should have a hollow sound when you tap on bottom and sides. Instant-read thermometer should register about 205°F. Store in refrigerator for up to 1 week or freezer for up to 10 days. Can be cut into 16 slices, not including ends.

Panini Sandwich Bread

The fragrant rosemary in this loaf reminds me of rustic flat bread, which I use to make panini—hence its name.

1. During **KNEAD** cycle: add 2 to 3 tablespoons chopped fresh rosemary when machine beeps and the ADD indicator flashes. Scrape the pan with a rubber spatula if flour and/or olives cling to the sides.

2. Optional: When the timer says 1:55 and the machine stops kneading, quickly sprinkle 1 to 2 tablespoons white cornmeal over top of bread.

Cook's Note:
Ideally, this bread should be about 3½ to 3¾ inches high in the very center of the loaf. The height of your bread may vary slightly. Refer to page 49 for more information.

Onion–Dill Sandwich Bread

Cook's Note:
Ideally, this bread should be about 3¼ to 3½ inches high in the very center of the loaf. The height of your bread may vary slightly. Refer to page 49 for more information.

Although this bread is delicious with just the onions, I choose to add fresh dill to enhance the flavor. It would also be delicious with 2 teaspoons fresh or 1 teaspoon dried thyme.

1. Heat 2 teaspoons canola oil in a heavy medium-sized skillet over medium heat. Stir in 1 cup finely diced onion and cook until softened, but not brown. Put onion in a small dish and set aside to cool. Make sure the mixture is not too wet.

2. During **KNEAD** cycle: add cooked onion and 1 tablespoon chopped fresh dill weed (optional) when machine beeps and the ADD indicator flashes. Scrape the pan with a rubber spatula if flour, onions, and/or dill cling to the sides.

Rosemary–Olive Sandwich Bread

Cook's Note:
Ideally, this bread should be about 3¼ to 3½ inches high in the very center of the loaf. The height of your bread may vary slightly. Refer to page 49 for more information.

You can make the Panini Sandwich Bread recipe on page 51 a little more exotic by adding delicious brine-cured olives to the mix.

1. During **KNEAD** cycle: add ¾ to 1 cup kalamata (or other brine-cured) olives and 1 to 2 tablespoons chopped fresh rosemary (optional) when machine beeps and the ADD indicator flashes. Scrape the pan with a rubber spatula if flour, olives, and/or rosemary cling to the sides.

Sun-Dried Tomato and Roasted Garlic Sandwich Bread

This loaf has a gentle garlic flavor that combines well with the sun-dried tomatoes. If you prefer a stronger garlic flavor, use 3 tablespoons minced garlic and 2 teaspoons olive oil instead of the amounts specified in the instructions.

1. Heat 1 teaspoon olive oil in a heavy small saucepan over medium heat. Turn heat to low, stir in 2 tablespoons minced garlic, and cook about 5 minutes until softened and cooked to a very light golden brown. Mix garlic with ½ to ¾ cup well-drained and chopped sun-dried tomatoes, packed in oil, in a small dish and set aside to cool.

2. During **KNEAD** cycle: add sun-dried tomatoes and mashed garlic mixture when machine beeps and the ADD indicator flashes. Scrape the pan with a rubber spatula if flour, sun-dried tomatoes, and/or garlic cling to the sides.

Cook's Note:
Ideally, this bread should be about 3 to 3½ inches high in the very center of the loaf. The height of your bread may vary slightly. Refer to page 49 for more information.

Parmesan Sandwich Bread

Cook's Note:
Ideally, this bread should be about 3 to 3½ inches high in the very center of the loaf. The height of your bread may vary slightly. Refer to page 49 for more information.

Much of the allure of cheese bread lies in its aroma, because unless the bread is a stuffed or filled version, there is usually only a hint of actual cheese flavor. Indeed, this bread does smell incredible when it is baking and will make a fragrant addition to your meal. It also makes great crostini and panini. Take note: you can substitute another kind of cheese, but make sure it is a cheese that is naturally lower in fat, such as Parmesan; high-fat cheeses give off too much moisture for this particular recipe.

1. During **KNEAD** cycle: add ¾ cup coarsely grated well-aged Parmesan cheese when machine beeps and the ADD indicator flashes. Scrape the pan with a rubber spatula if flour and/or cheese cling to the sides.

2. Optional: When the timer says 1:55 and the machine stops kneading, quickly sprinkle 1 tablespoon coarsely grated well-aged Parmesan cheese over top of bread.

Oatmeal Artisan Bread

Makes 1 loaf

Ground oatmeal enhances the chewiness of this very simple bread. A great everyday loaf for sandwiches and toast, it is a kid-pleasing favorite because of its sweet, nutty taste. I like to add sesame seeds to enrich the flavor (see recipe below), but you can add any other seeds you like.

1½ cups water (between 65°F and 75°F)

2 teaspoons canola oil (between 65°F and 75°F)

2⅔ cups Bread Flour Mix A (see page 6)

⅓ cup coarsely ground oatmeal

3 tablespoons sugar

2 teaspoons xanthan gum

1 teaspoon salt

1 packet (¼ ounce) active dry yeast granules (not quick-rise)

1. Set your Zojirushi bread machine to **HOME MADE – MEMORY 1** (see page 15). Press **Crust Control** until the arrow points to Dark**.**

2. Remove bread pan from machine and make sure kneading blades are firmly secured in place.

3. Whisk water and canola oil together in a glass measuring cup and pour into the bread pan.

4. Whisk Bread Flour Mix A, ground oatmeal, sugar, xanthan gum, salt, and yeast in a small mixing bowl or container until well combined

Cook's Notes:

Dry ingredients can be pre-mixed ahead of time and stored in plastic containers for future use. However, do not add yeast until you are just about to bake bread.

Ideally, this bread should be about 3 to 3½ inches high in the very center of the loaf. The height of your bread may vary slightly. Refer to page 49 for more information.

and sprinkle over the liquids. Without pressing down excessively hard, try to spread out the dry ingredients so they cover all the liquid.

5. Put the bread pan into the machine, secure it in place, and close the lid. Press **Start/Restart**.

6. Optional, but suggested: During **KNEAD** cycle, scrape the pan with a rubber spatula if flour clings to sides.

7. Remove bread pan from machine promptly when the **BAKE** cycle ends. Turn bread pan over to remove bread and place it on a rack to cool (use a rubber spatula to release it if it sticks so you don't scrap the nonstick pan). Bread should have a hollow sound when you tap on bottom and sides. Instant-read thermometer should register about 205°F. Store in refrigerator for up to 1 week or freezer for up to 10 days. Can be cut into 16 slices, not including ends.

Oatmeal–Sesame Artisan Bread

1. During **KNEAD** cycle: add 2 to 3 tablespoons sesame seeds when machine beeps and the ADD indicator flashes. Scrape the pan with a rubber spatula if flour and/or seeds cling to the sides.

Rye Artisan Bread

Makes 1 loaf

A chewy artisan-style rye bread hits the spot when you're in the mood for a change of pace. It makes wonderful toast for breakfast, a delectable sandwich, or a great grilled cheese. Gluten-free rye flavoring makes this very special bread a reality for those who want or need to avoid gluten-rich rye flour.

1½ cups water (between 65°F and 75°F)

2 teaspoons canola oil (between 65°F and 75°F)

2⅔ cups Bread Flour Mix A (see page 6)

⅓ cup teff flour

3 tablespoons sugar

2 teaspoons xanthan gum

1 teaspoon salt

1½ teaspoons rye flavor*

1 packet (¼ ounce) active dry yeast granules (not quick-rise)

2½–3 tablespoons caraway seeds (or to taste)

1. Set your Zojirushi bread machine to **HOME MADE – MEMORY 1** (see page 15). Press **Crust Control** until the arrow points to Dark.

2. Remove bread pan from machine and make sure kneading blades are firmly secured in place.

3. Whisk water and canola oil together in a glass measuring cup and pour into the bread pan.

4. Whisk Bread Flour Mix A, teff flour, sugar,

Cook's Notes:
Dry ingredients can be pre-mixed ahead of time and stored in plastic containers for future use. However, do not add yeast until you are just about to bake bread.

Ideally, this bread should be about 3½ to 3¾ inches high in the very center of the loaf. The height of your bread may vary slightly. Refer to page 49 for more information.

This bread has a classic New York deli–style rye taste. After you make it the first time, you can adjust the amount of rye flavor according to your preference. If you prefer it milder, decrease it in ½-teaspoon increments. For a stronger rye flavor, increase it in ½-teaspoon increments.

* An excellent gluten-free rye flavor is available from Authentic Foods (see page 12 for details).

xanthan gum, salt, rye flavor, and yeast in a small mixing bowl or container until well combined and sprinkle over the liquids. Without pressing down excessively hard, try to spread out the dry ingredients so they cover all the liquid.

5. Put the bread pan into the machine, secure it in place, and close the lid. Press **Start/Restart**.

6. During **KNEAD** cycle: add caraway seeds when machine beeps and the ADD indicator flashes. Scrape the pan with a rubber spatula if flour and/or seeds cling to the sides.

7. Remove bread pan from machine promptly when the **BAKE** cycle ends. Turn bread pan over to remove bread and place it on a rack to cool (use a rubber spatula to release the bread if it sticks, so you won't scrape the nonstick pan). Bread should have a hollow sound when you tap on bottom and sides. Instant-read thermometer should register about 205°F. Store in refrigerator for up to 1 week or freezer for up to 10 days. Can be cut into 16 slices, not including ends.

Cook's Note:
Ideally, this bread should be about 3¼ to 3½ inches high in the very center of the loaf. The height of your bread may vary slightly. Refer to page 49 for more information.

Black Forest Onion–Rye Artisan Bread

My grandmother came from the Black Forest region of Germany, and this bread, which is also called Zweibelbrot, reminds me of her. It makes nice moist slices for a delicious sandwich, and goes well alongside sausages, wursts, and mustards.

1. Melt 1 tablespoon butter or butter substitute in

a medium-sized frying pan over medium heat. Stir in 1 cup finely diced onion and cook until softened, but not browned. Put onions in a small dish and set aside to cool. Make sure the mixture is not too wet.

2.   During **KNEAD** cycle: add cooked onions (in addition to the 2½ to 3 tablespoons of caraway seeds) when machine beeps and the ADD indicator flashes. Scrape the pan with a rubber spatula if flour, onions, and/or seeds cling to the sides.

Swedish Rye Artisan Bread

A special loaf that blends a hint of orange with fragrant fennel or anise seed.

1.   During **KNEAD** cycle: add grated rind of 1 medium orange and substitute 1 to 2 teaspoons slightly crushed fennel or anise seed (to taste) for the caraway seed when machine beeps and the ADD indicator flashes. Scrape the pan with a rubber spatula if flour, orange rind, and/or seeds cling to the sides.

Cook's Note:
Ideally, this bread should be about 3½ to 3¾ inches high in the very center of the loaf. The height of your bread may vary slightly. Refer to page 49 for more information.

Pecan Artisan Bread

Makes 1 loaf

Luxuriate in the simplicity of this very remarkable bread. Sweet, nutty pecans enhance the taste and texture to make this a loaf you will look forward to making and eating over and over. The bread can be enjoyed for breakfast with jam and nut butters, and it is perfect with soup and salad. I like to make it into crisp, thin toast to serve with wine and cheese. The Pecan–Raisin Artisan Bread variation (recipe follows) is a particular favorite of mine.

1½ cups water (between 65°F and 75°F)

2 teaspoons canola oil (between 65°F and 75°F)

2⅔ cups Bread Flour Mix A (see page 6)

⅓ cup finely ground pecans

3 tablespoons sugar

2 teaspoons xanthan gum

1 teaspoon salt

1 packet (¼ ounce) active dry yeast granules (not quick-rise)

¾ cup chopped pecans

1. Set your Zojirushi bread machine to **HOME MADE – MEMORY 1** (see page 15). Press **Crust Control** until the arrow points to Dark.

2. Remove bread pan from machine and make sure kneading blades are firmly secured in place.

3. Whisk water and canola oil together in a glass measuring cup and pour into the bread pan.

Cook's Notes:

Dry ingredients can be pre-mixed ahead of time and stored in plastic containers for future use. However, do not add yeast until you are just about to bake bread.

Ideally, this bread should be about 3 to 3½ inches high in the very center of the loaf. The height of your bread may vary slightly. Refer to page 49 for more information.

4. Whisk Bread Flour Mix A, finely ground pecans, sugar, xanthan gum, salt, and yeast in a small mixing bowl or container until well combined and sprinkle over the liquids. Without pressing down excessively hard, try to spread out the dry ingredients so they cover all the liquid.

5. Put the bread pan into the machine, secure it in place, and close the lid. Press **Start/Restart**.

6. During **KNEAD** cycle: add ¾ cup chopped pecans when machine beeps and the ADD indicator flashes. Scrape the pan with a rubber spatula if flour and/or nuts cling to the sides.

7. Remove bread pan from machine promptly when the **BAKE** cycle ends. Turn bread pan over to remove bread and place it on a rack to cool (use a rubber spatula to release the bread if it sticks, so you won't scrape the nonstick pan). Bread should have a hollow sound when you tap on bottom and sides. Instant-read thermometer should register about 205°F. Store in refrigerator for up to 1 week or freezer for up to 10 days. Can be cut into 16 slices, not including ends.

Pecan–Raisin Artisan Bread

1. During **KNEAD** cycle: add ⅔ cup raisins (in addition to ⅔ cup chopped pecans) when machine beeps and the ADD indicator flashes. Scrape the pan with a rubber spatula if flour, raisins, and/or nuts cling to the sides.

Walnut Artisan Bread

Makes 1 loaf

The rich flavor of this fragrant walnut bread will win you over. It is delicious for breakfast alongside jams and nut butters, and it can help turn a simple soup or salad into something you can savor. I like to make it with raisins or dried cranberries (recipes follow) and serve toasted slices with a cheese course for a special treat.

Cook's Notes:

Dry ingredients can be pre-mixed ahead of time and stored in plastic containers for future use. However, do not add yeast until you are just about to bake bread.

Ideally, this bread should be about 3 to 3½ inches high in the very center of the loaf. The height of your bread may vary slightly. Refer to page 49 for more information.

1½ cups water (between 65°F and 75°F)

2 teaspoons canola oil (between 65°F and 75°F)

2⅔ cups Bread Flour Mix A (see page 6)

⅓ cup finely ground walnuts

3 tablespoons sugar

2 teaspoons xanthan gum

1 teaspoon salt

1 packet (¼ ounce) active dry yeast granules (not quick-rise)

¾ cup chopped walnuts

1. Set your Zojirushi bread machine to **HOME MADE – MEMORY 1** (see page 15). Press **Crust Control** until the arrow points to Dark.

2. Remove bread pan from machine and make sure kneading blades are firmly secured in place.

3. Whisk water and canola oil together in a glass measuring cup and pour into the bread pan.

4. Whisk Bread Flour Mix A, finely ground walnuts, sugar, xanthan gum, salt, and yeast in a small

mixing bowl or container until well combined and sprinkle over the liquids. Without pressing down excessively hard, try to spread out the dry ingredients so they cover all the liquid.

5. Put the bread pan into the machine, secure it in place, and close the lid. Press **Start/Restart**.

6. During **KNEAD** cycle: add ¾ cup chopped walnuts when machine beeps and the ADD indicator flashes. Scrape the pan with a rubber spatula if flour and/or nuts cling to the sides.

7. Remove bread pan from machine promptly when the **BAKE** cycle ends. Turn bread pan over to remove bread and place it on a rack to cool (use a rubber spatula to release the bread if it sticks, so you won't scrape the nonstick pan). Bread should have a hollow sound when you tap on bottom and sides. Instant-read thermometer should register about 205°F. Store in refrigerator for up to 1 week or freezer for up to 10 days. Can be cut into 16 slices, not including ends.

Walnut–Raisin Artisan Bread

1. During **KNEAD** cycle: add ⅔ cup raisins (in addition to ⅔ cup chopped walnuts) when machine beeps and the ADD indicator flashes. Scrape the pan with a rubber spatula if flour, raisins, and/or nuts cling to the sides.

Cranberry–Walnut Yeast Artisan Bread

1. During **KNEAD** cycle: add ⅔ cup dried cranberries (in addition to ⅔ cup chopped walnuts) when machine beeps and the ADD indicator flashes. Scrape the pan with a rubber spatula if flour, cranberries, and/or nuts cling to the sides.

Multi-Grain Artisan Bread

Makes 1 loaf

Yearning for a hearty, flavorful bread? I substitute teff flour for some of the Bread Flour Mix A in this recipe to create a multi-grain loaf that will remind you of the artisan whole-wheat loaves you left behind. If you prefer, you can add Montina, quinoa, or amaranth in place of the teff. I also toss in sesame seeds, sunflower seeds, and golden flax seeds to enhance the loaf's taste and texture, but you can add any combination of seeds you want—up to 6 tablespoons (don't add more, or your bread will be too dense). Try the nut versions (recipes follow) to create more delicious variations.

Cook's Notes:
Dry ingredients can be pre-mixed ahead of time and stored in plastic containers for future use. However, do not add yeast until you are just about to bake bread.

Ideally, this bread should be about 3 to 3½ inches high in the very center of the loaf. The height of your bread may vary slightly. Refer to page 49 for more information.

1½ cups water (between 65°F and 75°F)

2 teaspoons olive oil (between 65°F and 75°F)

2⅔ cups Bread Flour Mix A (see page 6)

⅓ cup teff flour

3 tablespoons sugar

2 teaspoons xanthan gum

1 teaspoon salt

1 packet (¼ ounce) active dry yeast granules (not quick-rise)

2 tablespoons sesame seeds

2 tablespoons flax seed

2 tablespoons sunflower seeds

1. Set your Zojirushi bread machine to **HOME MADE – MEMORY 1** (see page 15). Press **Crust Control** until the arrow points to Dark.

2. Remove bread pan from machine and make sure kneading blades are firmly secured in place.

3. Whisk water and olive oil together in a glass measuring cup and pour into the bread pan.

4. Whisk Bread Flour Mix A, teff flour, sugar, xanthan gum, salt, and yeast in a small mixing bowl or container until well combined and sprinkle over the liquids. Without pressing down excessively hard, try to spread out the dry ingredients so they cover all the liquid.

5. Put the bread pan into the machine, secure it in place, and close the lid. Press **Start/Restart**.

6. During **KNEAD** cycle: add sesame, flax, and sunflower seeds when machine beeps and the ADD indicator flashes. Scrape the pan with a rubber spatula if flour and/or seeds cling to the sides.

7. Remove bread pan from machine promptly when the **BAKE** cycle ends. Turn bread pan over to remove bread and place it on a rack to cool (use a rubber spatula to release the bread if it sticks, so you won't scrape the nonstick pan). Bread should have a hollow sound when you tap on bottom and sides. Instant-read thermometer should register about 205°F. Store in refrigerator for up to 1 week or freezer for up to 10 days. Can be cut into 16 slices, not including ends.

Multi-Grain Pecan Artisan Bread

1. During **KNEAD** cycle: add ¾ cup chopped pecans (and up to 2 tablespoons seeds, if desired) when

machine beeps and the ADD indicator flashes. Scrape the pan with a rubber spatula if flour and/or nuts cling to the sides.

Multi-Grain Walnut Artisan Bread

1. During **KNEAD** cycle: add ¾ cup chopped walnuts (and up to 2 tablespoons seeds, if desired) when machine beeps and the ADD indicator flashes. Scrape the pan with a rubber spatula if flour and/or nuts cling to the sides.

Golden Italian Artisan Bread with Raisins and Fennel

Dry ingredients
can be pre-mixed
ahead of time
and stored in
plastic containers
for future use.
However, do not
add yeast until you
are just about to
bake bread.

Ideally, this bread
should be about
3½ to 3¾ inches
high in the very
center of the loaf.
The height of your
bread may vary
slightly. Refer to
page 49 for more
information.

Makes 1 loaf

After I moved away from New York City, I would make special trips back just to buy the wheat version of this incredible artisan bread. It was called "Semolina with Golden Raisins and Fennel," and it was the signature bread of Amy's Bread, a bakery started by the very talented Amy Scherber in 1992. I had just about given up on ever tasting it again, but then I unlocked the key to making a good gluten-free French–Italian bread. It was just a matter of time before I added the golden raisins and fennel seeds I longed for. Although this bread-machine version lacks the crusty exterior of my oven-baked version, it retains the chewy, flavorful spirit of the original. In order to create the same golden glow without semolina flour, dust the top of the loaf with yellow cornmeal (Amy dusts her bread with cornmeal as well). Even if you weren't fortunate enough to taste the original, you'll come to crave this delicious gluten-free copy.

1½ cups water (between 65°F and 75°F)

1 tablespoon olive oil (between 65°F and 75°F)

3 cups Bread Flour Mix A (see page 6)

3 tablespoons sugar

2 teaspoons xanthan gum

1 teaspoon salt

1 packet (¼ ounce) active dry yeast granules (not quick-rise)

1 cup golden raisins

2–3 teaspoons fennel seeds

1–2 tablespoons yellow cornmeal

1. Set your Zojirushi bread machine to **HOME MADE – MEMORY 1** (see page 15). Press **Crust Control** until the arrow points to Dark.

2. Remove bread pan from machine and make sure kneading blades are firmly secured in place.

3. Whisk water and olive oil in a glass measuring cup and pour into the bread pan.

4. Whisk Bread Flour Mix A, sugar, xanthan gum, salt, and yeast in a small mixing bowl or container until well combined and sprinkle over the liquids. Without pressing down excessively hard, try to spread out the dry ingredients so they cover all the liquid.

5. Put the bread pan into the machine, secure it in place, and close the lid. Press **Start/Restart**.

6. During **KNEAD** cycle: add 1 cup golden raisins and 2 to 3 teaspoons fennel seeds when machine beeps and the ADD indicator flashes. Scrape the pan with a rubber spatula if flour, raisins, and/or seeds cling to the sides.

7. When the timer says 1:55 and the machine stops kneading, quickly sprinkle yellow cornmeal over top of bread.

8. Remove bread pan from machine promptly when the **BAKE** cycle ends. Turn bread pan over to remove bread and place it on a rack to cool (use a rubber spatula to release the bread if it sticks, so you won't scrape the nonstick pan). Bread should have a hollow sound when you tap on bottom and sides. Instant-read thermometer should register about 205°F. Store in refrigerator for up to 1 week or freezer for up to 10 days. Can be cut into 16 slices, not including ends.

Index